AF808553

AGENDA

YEAR

FULL NAME:

PHONE NUMBER:

EMAIL:

HW
HILL WEISER
PUBLISHING

JANUARY EXPENSES

EXPENSES	AMOUNT	DATE

JANUARY GOALS

GOALS	DATE	DONE

JANUARY / /

S M T W T F S

PRIORITIES

TO-DO

TIME

DAILIES

MEALS

B

L

D

S

JANUARY / /

S M T W T F S

PRIORITIES

TO-DO

TIME

DAILIES

MEALS

B

L

D

S

JANUARY / /

S M T W T F S

PRIORITIES

TO-DO

TIME

DAILIES

MEALS

B

L

D

S

JANUARY / /

S M T W T F S

PRIORITIES

TO-DO

TIME

DAILIES

MEALS

B

L

D

S

JANUARY /   /

S M T W T F S

PRIORITIES

TO-DO

TIME

DAILIES

MEALS

B

L

D

S

JANUARY / /

S M T W T F S

PRIORITIES

TO-DO

TIME

DAILIES

MEALS

B

L

D

S

JANUARY / /

S M T W T F S

PRIORITIES

TO-DO

TIME

DAILIES

MEALS

B

L

D

S

JANUARY / /

S M T W T F S

PRIORITIES

TO-DO

TIME

DAILIES

MEALS

B

L

D

S

JANUARY / /

S M T W T F S

PRIORITIES

TO-DO

TIME

DAILIES

MEALS

B

L

D

S

JANUARY / /

S M T W T F S

PRIORITIES

TO-DO

TIME

DAILIES

MEALS

B

L

D

S

JANUARY / /

S M T W T F S

PRIORITIES

TO-DO

TIME

DAILIES

MEALS

B

L

D

S

JANUARY / /

S M T W T F S

PRIORITIES

TO-DO

TIME

DAILIES

MEALS

B

L

D

S

JANUARY / /

S M T W T F S

PRIORITIES

TO-DO

TIME

DAILIES

MEALS

B

L

D

S

JANUARY / /

S M T W T F S

PRIORITIES

TO-DO

TIME

DAILIES

MEALS

B

L

D

S

JANUARY / /

S M T W T F S

PRIORITIES

TO-DO

TIME

DAILIES

MEALS

B

L

D

S

JANUARY /   /

S M T W T F S

PRIORITIES

TO-DO

TIME

DAILIES

MEALS

B

L

D

S

JANUARY / /

S M T W T F S

PRIORITIES

TO-DO

TIME

DAILIES

MEALS

B

L

D

S

JANUARY / /

S M T W T F S

PRIORITIES

TO-DO

TIME

DAILIES

MEALS

B

L

D

S

JANUARY / /

S M T W T F S

PRIORITIES

TO-DO

TIME

DAILIES

MEALS

B

L

D

S

JANUARY / /

S M T W T F S

PRIORITIES

TO-DO

TIME

DAILIES

MEALS

B

L

D

S

JANUARY / /

S M T W T F S

PRIORITIES

TO-DO

TIME

DAILIES

MEALS

B

L

D

S

JANUARY / /

S M T W T F S

PRIORITIES

TO-DO

TIME

DAILIES

MEALS

B

L

D

S

JANUARY / /

S M T W T F S

PRIORITIES

TO-DO

TIME

DAILIES

MEALS

B

L

D

S

JANUARY / /

S M T W T F S

PRIORITIES

TO-DO

TIME

DAILIES

MEALS

B

L

D

S

JANUARY / /

S M T W T F S

PRIORITIES

TO-DO

TIME

DAILIES

MEALS

B

L

D

S

JANUARY / /

S M T W T F S

PRIORITIES

TO-DO

TIME

DAILIES

MEALS

B

L

D

S

JANUARY / /

S M T W T F S

PRIORITIES

TO-DO

TIME

DAILIES

MEALS

B

L

D

S

JANUARY /   /

S M T W T F S

PRIORITIES

TO-DO

TIME

DAILIES

MEALS

B

L

D

S

JANUARY / /

S M T W T F S

PRIORITIES

TO-DO

TIME

DAILIES

MEALS

B

L

D

S

JANUARY / /

S M T W T F S

PRIORITIES

TO-DO

TIME

DAILIES

MEALS

B

L

D

S

JANUARY / /

S M T W T F S

PRIORITIES

TO-DO

TIME

DAILIES

MEALS

B

L

D

S

JANUARY REVIEW

Summary of this Month's Accomplishments

FEBRUARY EXPENSES

EXPENSES	AMOUNT	DATE

FEBRUARY GOALS

GOALS	DATE	DONE

FEBRUARY / /

S M T W T F S

PRIORITIES

TO-DO

TIME

DAILIES

MEALS

B

L

D

S

FEBRUARY / /

S M T W T F S

PRIORITIES

TO-DO

TIME

DAILIES

MEALS

B

L

D

S

FEBRUARY / /

S M T W T F S

PRIORITIES

TO-DO

TIME

DAILIES

MEALS

B

L

D

S

FEBRUARY / /

S M T W T F S

PRIORITIES

TO-DO

TIME

DAILIES

MEALS

B

L

D

S

FEBRUARY / /

S M T W T F S

PRIORITIES

TO-DO

TIME

DAILIES

MEALS

B

L

D

S

FEBRUARY / /

S M T W T F S

PRIORITIES

TO-DO

TIME

DAILIES

MEALS

B

L

D

S

FEBRUARY / /

S M T W T F S

PRIORITIES

TO-DO

TIME

DAILIES

MEALS

B

L

D

S

FEBRUARY / /

S M T W T F S

PRIORITIES

TO-DO

TIME

DAILIES

MEALS

B

L

D

S

FEBRUARY / /

S M T W T F S

PRIORITIES

TO-DO

TIME

DAILIES

MEALS

B

L

D

S

FEBRUARY / /

S M T W T F S

PRIORITIES

TO-DO

TIME

DAILIES

MEALS

B

L

D

S

FEBRUARY / /

S M T W T F S

PRIORITIES

TO-DO

TIME

DAILIES

MEALS

B

L

D

S

FEBRUARY /   /

S M T W T F S

PRIORITIES

TO-DO

TIME

DAILIES

MEALS

B

L

D

S

FEBRUARY / /

S M T W T F S

PRIORITIES

TO-DO

TIME

DAILIES

MEALS

B

L

D

S

FEBRUARY / /

S M T W T F S

PRIORITIES

TO-DO

TIME

DAILIES

MEALS

B

L

D

S

FEBRUARY /   /

S M T W T F S

PRIORITIES

TO-DO

TIME

DAILIES

MEALS

B

L

D

S

FEBRUARY / /

S M T W T F S

PRIORITIES

TO-DO

TIME

DAILIES

MEALS

B

L

D

S

FEBRUARY / /

S M T W T F S

PRIORITIES

TO-DO

TIME

DAILIES

MEALS

B

L

D

S

FEBRUARY / /

S M T W T F S

PRIORITIES

TO-DO

TIME

DAILIES

MEALS

B

L

D

S

FEBRUARY / /

S M T W T F S

PRIORITIES

TO-DO

TIME

DAILIES

MEALS

B

L

D

S

FEBRUARY / /

S M T W T F S

PRIORITIES

TO-DO

TIME

DAILIES

MEALS

B

L

D

S

FEBRUARY /   /

S M T W T F S

PRIORITIES

TO-DO

TIME

DAILIES

MEALS

B

L

D

S

FEBRUARY / /

S M T W T F S

PRIORITIES

TO-DO

TIME

DAILIES

MEALS

B

L

D

S

FEBRUARY / /

S M T W T F S

PRIORITIES

TO-DO

TIME

DAILIES

MEALS

B

L

D

S

FEBRUARY / /

S M T W T F S

PRIORITIES

TO-DO

TIME

DAILIES

MEALS

B

L

D

S

FEBRUARY / /

S M T W T F S

PRIORITIES

TO-DO

TIME

DAILIES

MEALS

B

L

D

S

FEBRUARY / /

S M T W T F S

PRIORITIES

TO-DO

TIME

DAILIES

MEALS

B

L

D

S

FEBRUARY / /

S M T W T F S

PRIORITIES

TO-DO

TIME

DAILIES

MEALS

B

L

D

S

FEBRUARY / /

S M T W T F S

PRIORITIES

TO-DO

TIME

DAILIES

MEALS

B

L

D

S

FEBRUARY / /

S M T W T F S

PRIORITIES

TO-DO

TIME

DAILIES

MEALS

B

L

D

S

FEBRUARY REVIEW

Summary of this Month's Accomplishments

MARCH EXPENSES

EXPENSES	AMOUNT	DATE

MARCH GOALS

GOALS	DATE	DONE

MARCH / /

S M T W T F S

PRIORITIES

TO-DO

TIME

DAILIES

MEALS

B

L

D

S

MARCH / /

S M T W T F S

PRIORITIES

TO-DO

TIME

DAILIES

MEALS

B

L

D

S

MARCH /   /

S M T W T F S

PRIORITIES

TO-DO

TIME

DAILIES

MEALS

B

L

D

S

MARCH / /

S M T W T F S

PRIORITIES

TO-DO

TIME

DAILIES

MEALS

B

L

D

S

MARCH / /

S M T W T F S

PRIORITIES

TO-DO

TIME

DAILIES

MEALS

B

L

D

S

MARCH / /

S M T W T F S

PRIORITIES

TO-DO

TIME

DAILIES

MEALS

B

L

D

S

MARCH / /

S M T W T F S

PRIORITIES

TO-DO

TIME

DAILIES

MEALS

B

L

D

S

MARCH / /

S M T W T F S

PRIORITIES

TO-DO

TIME

DAILIES

MEALS

B

L

D

S

MARCH / /

S M T W T F S

PRIORITIES

TO-DO

TIME

DAILIES

MEALS

B

L

D

S

MARCH /   /

S M T W T F S

PRIORITIES

TO-DO

TIME

DAILIES

MEALS

B

L

D

S

MARCH / /

S M T W T F S

PRIORITIES

TO-DO

TIME

DAILIES

MEALS

B

L

D

S

MARCH / /

S M T W T F S

PRIORITIES

TO-DO

TIME

DAILIES

MEALS

B

L

D

S

MARCH /   /

S M T W T F S

PRIORITIES

TO-DO

TIME

DAILIES

MEALS

B

L

D

S

MARCH / /

S M T W T F S

PRIORITIES

TO-DO

TIME

DAILIES

MEALS

B

L

D

S

MARCH / /

S M T W T F S

PRIORITIES

TO-DO

TIME

DAILIES

MEALS

B

L

D

S

MARCH / /

S M T W T F S

PRIORITIES

TO-DO

TIME

DAILIES

MEALS

B

L

D

S

MARCH / /

S M T W T F S

PRIORITIES

TO-DO

TIME

DAILIES

MEALS

B

L

D

S

MARCH / /

S M T W T F S

PRIORITIES

TO-DO

TIME

DAILIES

MEALS

B

L

D

S

MARCH / /

S M T W T F S

PRIORITIES

TO-DO

TIME

DAILIES

MEALS

B

L

D

S

MARCH / /

S M T W T F S

PRIORITIES

TO-DO

TIME

DAILIES

MEALS

B

L

D

S

MARCH / /

S M T W T F S

PRIORITIES

TO-DO

TIME

DAILIES

MEALS

B

L

D

S

MARCH / /

S M T W T F S

PRIORITIES

TO-DO

TIME

DAILIES

MEALS

B

L

D

S

MARCH / /

S M T W T F S

PRIORITIES

TO-DO

TIME

DAILIES

MEALS

B

L

D

S

MARCH / /

S M T W T F S

PRIORITIES

TO-DO

TIME

DAILIES

MEALS

B

L

D

S

MARCH /   /

S M T W T F S

PRIORITIES

TO-DO

TIME

DAILIES

MEALS

B

L

D

S

MARCH / /

S M T W T F S

PRIORITIES

TO-DO

TIME

DAILIES

MEALS

B

L

D

S

MARCH / /

S M T W T F S

PRIORITIES

TO-DO

TIME

DAILIES

MEALS

B

L

D

S

MARCH / /

S M T W T F S

PRIORITIES

TO-DO

TIME

DAILIES

MEALS

B

L

D

S

MARCH / /

S M T W T F S

PRIORITIES

TO-DO

TIME

DAILIES

MEALS

B

L

D

S

MARCH / /

S M T W T F S

PRIORITIES

TO-DO

TIME

DAILIES

MEALS

B

L

D

S

MARCH /   /

S M T W T F S

PRIORITIES

TO-DO

TIME

DAILIES

MEALS

B

L

D

S

MARCH REVIEW

Summary of this Month's Accomplishments

APRIL EXPENSES

EXPENSES	AMOUNT	DATE

APRIL GOALS

GOALS	DATE	DONE

APRIL / /

S M T W T F S

PRIORITIES

TO-DO

TIME

DAILIES

MEALS

B

L

D

S

APRIL / /

S M T W T F S

PRIORITIES

TO-DO

TIME

DAILIES

MEALS

B

L

D

S

APRIL / /

S M T W T F S

PRIORITIES

TO-DO

TIME

DAILIES

MEALS

B

L

D

S

APRIL /　　/

S M T W T F S

PRIORITIES

TO-DO

TIME

DAILIES

MEALS

B

L

D

S

APRIL / /

S M T W T F S

PRIORITIES

TO-DO

TIME

DAILIES

MEALS

B

L

D

S

APRIL / /

S M T W T F S

PRIORITIES

TO-DO

TIME

DAILIES

MEALS

B

L

D

S

APRIL / /

S M T W T F S

PRIORITIES

TO-DO

TIME

DAILIES

MEALS

B

L

D

S

APRIL / /

S M T W T F S

PRIORITIES

TO-DO

TIME

DAILIES

MEALS

B

L

D

S

APRIL / /

S M T W T F S

PRIORITIES

TO-DO

TIME

DAILIES

MEALS

B

L

D

S

APRIL / /

S M T W T F S

PRIORITIES

TO-DO

TIME

DAILIES

MEALS

B

L

D

S

APRIL / /

S M T W T F S

PRIORITIES

TO-DO

TIME

DAILIES

MEALS

B

L

D

S

APRIL / /

S M T W T F S

PRIORITIES

TO-DO

TIME

DAILIES

MEALS

B

L

D

S

APRIL / /

S M T W T F S

PRIORITIES

TO-DO

TIME

DAILIES

MEALS

B

L

D

S

APRIL / /

S M T W T F S

PRIORITIES

TO-DO

TIME

DAILIES

MEALS

B

L

D

S

APRIL / /

S M T W T F S

PRIORITIES

TO-DO

TIME

DAILIES

MEALS

B

L

D

S

APRIL / /

S M T W T F S

PRIORITIES

TO-DO

TIME

DAILIES

MEALS

B

L

D

S

APRIL /   /

S M T W T F S

PRIORITIES

TO-DO

TIME

DAILIES

MEALS

B

L

D

S

APRIL / /

S M T W T F S

PRIORITIES

TO-DO

TIME

DAILIES

MEALS

B

L

D

S

APRIL / /

S M T W T F S

PRIORITIES

TO-DO

TIME

DAILIES

MEALS

B

L

D

S

APRIL / /

S M T W T F S

PRIORITIES

TO-DO

TIME

DAILIES

MEALS

B

L

D

S

APRIL / /

S M T W T F S

PRIORITIES

TO-DO

TIME

DAILIES

MEALS

B

L

D

S

APRIL /   /

S M T W T F S

PRIORITIES

TO-DO

TIME

DAILIES

MEALS

B

L

D

S

APRIL / /

S M T W T F S

PRIORITIES

TO-DO

TIME

DAILIES

MEALS

B

L

D

S

APRIL / /

S M T W T F S

PRIORITIES

TO-DO

TIME

DAILIES

MEALS

B

L

D

S

APRIL / /

S M T W T F S

PRIORITIES

TO-DO

TIME

DAILIES

MEALS

B

L

D

S

APRIL / /

S M T W T F S

PRIORITIES

TO-DO

TIME

DAILIES

MEALS

B

L

D

S

APRIL / /

S M T W T F S

PRIORITIES

TO-DO

TIME

DAILIES

MEALS

B

L

D

S

APRIL / /

S M T W T F S

PRIORITIES

TO-DO

TIME

DAILIES

MEALS

B

L

D

S

APRIL / /

S M T W T F S

PRIORITIES

TO-DO

TIME

DAILIES

MEALS

B

L

D

S

APRIL / /

S M T W T F S

PRIORITIES

TO-DO

TIME

DAILIES

MEALS

B

L

D

S

APRIL REVIEW

Summary of this Month's Accomplishments

MAY EXPENSES

EXPENSES	AMOUNT	DATE

MAY GOALS

GOALS	DATE	DONE

MAY / /

S M T W T F S

PRIORITIES

TO-DO

TIME

DAILIES

MEALS

B

L

D

S

MAY / /

S M T W T F S

PRIORITIES

TO-DO

TIME

DAILIES

MEALS

B

L

D

S

MAY / /

S M T W T F S

PRIORITIES

TO-DO

TIME

DAILIES

MEALS

B

L

D

S

MAY / /

S M T W T F S

PRIORITIES

TO-DO

TIME

DAILIES

MEALS

B

L

D

S

MAY / /

S M T W T F S

PRIORITIES

TO-DO

TIME

DAILIES

MEALS

B

L

D

S

MAY / /

S M T W T F S

PRIORITIES

TO-DO

TIME

DAILIES

MEALS

B

L

D

S

MAY / /

S M T W T F S

PRIORITIES

TO-DO

TIME

DAILIES

MEALS

B

L

D

S

MAY / /

S M T W T F S

PRIORITIES

TO-DO

TIME

DAILIES

MEALS

B

L

D

S

MAY / /

S M T W T F S

PRIORITIES

TO-DO

TIME

DAILIES

MEALS

B

L

D

S

MAY / /

S M T W T F S

PRIORITIES

TO-DO

TIME

DAILIES

MEALS

B

L

D

S

MAY / /

S M T W T F S

PRIORITIES

TO-DO

TIME

DAILIES

MEALS

B

L

D

S

MAY / /

S M T W T F S

PRIORITIES

TO-DO

TIME

DAILIES

MEALS

B

L

D

S

MAY / /

S M T W T F S

PRIORITIES

TO-DO

TIME

DAILIES

MEALS

B

L

D

S

MAY / /

S M T W T F S

PRIORITIES

TO-DO

TIME

DAILIES

MEALS

B

L

D

S

MAY / /

S M T W T F S

PRIORITIES

TO-DO

TIME

DAILIES

MEALS

B

L

D

S

MAY / /

S M T W T F S

PRIORITIES

TO-DO

TIME

DAILIES

MEALS

B

L

D

S

MAY / /

S M T W T F S

PRIORITIES

TO-DO

TIME

DAILIES

MEALS

B

L

D

S

MAY / /

S M T W T F S

PRIORITIES

TO-DO

TIME

DAILIES

MEALS

B

L

D

S

MAY / /

S M T W T F S

PRIORITIES

TO-DO

TIME

DAILIES

MEALS

B

L

D

S

MAY /   /

S M T W T F S

PRIORITIES

TO-DO

TIME

DAILIES

MEALS

B

L

D

S

MAY / /

S M T W T F S

PRIORITIES

TO-DO

TIME

DAILIES

MEALS

B

L

D

S

MAY / /

S M T W T F S

PRIORITIES

TO-DO

TIME

DAILIES

MEALS

B

L

D

S

MAY / /

S M T W T F S

PRIORITIES

TO-DO

TIME

DAILIES

MEALS

B

L

D

S

MAY / /

S M T W T F S

PRIORITIES

TO-DO

TIME

DAILIES

MEALS

B

L

D

S

MAY / /

S M T W T F S

PRIORITIES

TO-DO

TIME

DAILIES

MEALS

B

L

D

S

MAY / /

S M T W T F S

PRIORITIES

TO-DO

TIME

DAILIES

MEALS

B

L

D

S

MAY / /

S M T W T F S

PRIORITIES

TO-DO

TIME

DAILIES

MEALS

B

L

D

S

MAY / /

S M T W T F S

PRIORITIES

TO-DO

TIME

DAILIES

MEALS

B

L

D

S

MAY / /

S M T W T F S

PRIORITIES

TO-DO

TIME

DAILIES

MEALS

B

L

D

S

MAY / /

S M T W T F S

PRIORITIES

TO-DO

TIME

DAILIES

MEALS

B

L

D

S

MAY / /

S M T W T F S

PRIORITIES

TO-DO

TIME

DAILIES

MEALS

B

L

D

S

MAY REVIEW

Summary of this Month's Accomplishments

JUNE EXPENSES

EXPENSES	AMOUNT	DATE

JUNE GOALS

GOALS	DATE	DONE

JUNE / /

S M T W T F S

PRIORITIES

TO-DO

TIME

DAILIES

MEALS

B

L

D

S

JUNE / /

S M T W T F S

PRIORITIES

TO-DO

TIME

DAILIES

MEALS

B

L

D

S

JUNE / /

S M T W T F S

PRIORITIES

TO-DO

TIME

DAILIES

MEALS

B

L

D

S

JUNE / /

S M T W T F S

PRIORITIES

TO-DO

TIME

DAILIES

MEALS

B

L

D

S

JUNE / /

S M T W T F S

PRIORITIES

TO-DO

TIME

DAILIES

MEALS

B

L

D

S

JUNE / /

S M T W T F S

PRIORITIES

TO-DO

TIME

DAILIES

MEALS

B

L

D

S

JUNE / /

S M T W T F S

PRIORITIES

TO-DO

TIME

DAILIES

MEALS

B

L

D

S

JUNE / /

S M T W T F S

PRIORITIES

TO-DO

TIME

DAILIES

MEALS

B

L

D

S

JUNE / /

S M T W T F S

PRIORITIES

TO-DO

TIME

DAILIES

MEALS

B

L

D

S

JUNE / /

S M T W T F S

PRIORITIES

TO-DO

TIME

DAILIES

MEALS

B

L

D

S

JUNE / /

S M T W T F S

PRIORITIES

TO-DO

TIME

DAILIES

MEALS

B

L

D

S

JUNE / /

S M T W T F S

PRIORITIES

TO-DO

TIME

DAILIES

MEALS

B

L

D

S

JUNE / /

S M T W T F S

PRIORITIES

TO-DO

TIME

DAILIES

MEALS

B

L

D

S

JUNE / /

S M T W T F S

PRIORITIES

TO-DO

TIME

DAILIES

MEALS

B

L

D

S

JUNE /   /

S M T W T F S

PRIORITIES

TO-DO

TIME

DAILIES

MEALS

B

L

D

S

JUNE / /

S M T W T F S

PRIORITIES

TO-DO

TIME

DAILIES

MEALS

B

L

D

S

JUNE / /

S M T W T F S

PRIORITIES

TO-DO

TIME

DAILIES

MEALS

B

L

D

S

JUNE / /

S M T W T F S

PRIORITIES

TO-DO

TIME

DAILIES

MEALS

B

L

D

S

JUNE / /

S M T W T F S

PRIORITIES

TO-DO

TIME

DAILIES

MEALS

B

L

D

S

JUNE /   /

S M T W T F S

PRIORITIES

TO-DO

TIME

DAILIES

MEALS

B

L

D

S

JUNE / /

S M T W T F S

PRIORITIES

TO-DO

TIME

DAILIES

MEALS

B

L

D

S

JUNE / /

S M T W T F S

PRIORITIES

TO-DO

TIME

DAILIES

MEALS

B

L

D

S

JUNE / /

S M T W T F S

PRIORITIES

TO-DO

TIME

DAILIES

MEALS

B

L

D

S

JUNE / /

S M T W T F S

PRIORITIES

TO-DO

TIME

DAILIES

MEALS

B

L

D

S

JUNE / /

S M T W T F S

PRIORITIES

TO-DO

TIME

DAILIES

MEALS

S

L

D

S

JUNE / /

S M T W T F S

PRIORITIES

TO-DO

TIME

DAILIES

MEALS

B

L

D

S

JUNE / /

S M T W T F S

PRIORITIES

TO-DO

TIME

DAILIES

MEALS

B

L

D

S

JUNE / /

S M T W T F S

PRIORITIES

TO-DO

TIME

DAILIES

MEALS

B

L

D

S

JUNE /   /

S M T W T F S

PRIORITIES

TO-DO

TIME

DAILIES

MEALS

B

L

D

S

JUNE / /

S M T W T F S

PRIORITIES

TO-DO

TIME

DAILIES

MEALS

B

L

D

S

JUNE REVIEW

Summary of this Month's Accomplishments

JULY EXPENSES

EXPENSES	AMOUNT	DATE

JULY GOALS

GOALS	DATE	DONE

JULY / /

S M T W T F S

PRIORITIES

TO-DO

TIME

DAILIES

MEALS

B

L

D

S

JULY /   /

S M T W T F S

PRIORITIES

TO-DO

TIME

DAILIES

MEALS

B

L

D

S

JULY / /

S M T W T F S

PRIORITIES

TO-DO

TIME

DAILIES

MEALS

B

L

D

S

JULY / /

S M T W T F S

PRIORITIES

TO-DO

TIME

DAILIES

MEALS

B

L

D

S

JULY / /

S M T W T F S

PRIORITIES

TO-DO

TIME

DAILIES

MEALS

B

L

D

S

JULY / /

S M T W T F S

PRIORITIES

TO-DO

TIME

DAILIES

MEALS

B

L

D

S

JULY / /

S M T W T F S

PRIORITIES

TO-DO

TIME

DAILIES

MEALS

B

L

D

S

JULY / /

S M T W T F S

PRIORITIES

TO-DO

TIME

DAILIES

MEALS

B

L

D

S

JULY / /

S M T W T F S

PRIORITIES

TO-DO

TIME

DAILIES

MEALS

B

L

D

S

JULY / /

S M T W T F S

PRIORITIES

TO-DO

TIME

DAILIES

MEALS

B

L

D

S

JULY / /

S M T W T F S

PRIORITIES

TO-DO

TIME

DAILIES

MEALS

B

L

D

S

JULY /   /

S M T W T F S

PRIORITIES

TO-DO

TIME

DAILIES

MEALS

B

L

D

S

JULY / /

S M T W T F S

PRIORITIES

TO-DO

TIME

DAILIES

MEALS

B

L

D

S

JULY /   /

S M T W T F S

PRIORITIES

TO-DO

TIME

DAILIES

MEALS

B

L

D

S

JULY / /

S M T W T F S

PRIORITIES

TO-DO

TIME

DAILIES

MEALS

B

L

D

S

JULY / /

S M T W T F S

PRIORITIES

TO-DO

TIME

DAILIES

MEALS

B

L

D

S

JULY / /

S M T W T F S

PRIORITIES

TO-DO

TIME

DAILIES

MEALS

B

L

D

S

JULY / /

S M T W T F S

PRIORITIES

TO-DO

TIME

DAILIES

MEALS

B

L

D

S

JULY / /

S M T W T F S

PRIORITIES

TO-DO

TIME

DAILIES

MEALS

B

L

D

S

JULY / /

S M T W T F S

PRIORITIES

TO-DO

TIME

DAILIES

MEALS

B

L

D

S

JULY / /

S M T W T F S

PRIORITIES

TO-DO

TIME

DAILIES

MEALS

B

L

D

S

JULY / /

S M T W T F S

PRIORITIES

TO-DO

TIME

DAILIES

MEALS

B

L

D

S

JULY / /

S M T W T F S

PRIORITIES

TO-DO

TIME

DAILIES

MEALS

B

L

D

S

JULY / /

S M T W T F S

PRIORITIES

TO-DO

TIME

DAILIES

MEALS

B

L

D

S

JULY / /

S M T W T F S

PRIORITIES

TO-DO

TIME

DAILIES

MEALS

B

L

D

S

JULY / /

S M T W T F S

PRIORITIES

TO-DO

TIME

DAILIES

MEALS

B

L

D

S

JULY / /

S M T W T F S

PRIORITIES

TO-DO

TIME

DAILIES

MEALS

B

L

D

S

JULY / /

S M T W T F S

PRIORITIES

TO-DO

TIME

DAILIES

MEALS

B

L

D

S

JULY / /

S M T W T F S

PRIORITIES

TO-DO

TIME

DAILIES

MEALS

B

L

D

S

JULY /   /

S M T W T F S

PRIORITIES

TO-DO

TIME

DAILIES

MEALS

B

L

D

S

JULY / /

S M T W T F S

PRIORITIES

TO-DO

TIME

DAILIES

MEALS

B

L

D

S

JULY REVIEW

Summary of this Month's Accomplishments

AUGUST EXPENSES

EXPENSES	AMOUNT	DATE

AUGUST GOALS

GOALS	DATE	DONE

AUGUST / /

S M T W T F S

PRIORITIES

TO-DO

TIME

DAILIES

MEALS

B

L

D

S

AUGUST /   /

S M T W T F S

PRIORITIES

TO-DO

TIME

DAILIES

MEALS

B

L

D

S

AUGUST / /

S M T W T F S

PRIORITIES

TO-DO

TIME

DAILIES

MEALS

B

L

D

S

AUGUST / /

S M T W T F S

PRIORITIES

TO-DO

TIME

DAILIES

MEALS

B

L

D

S

AUGUST / /

S M T W T F S

PRIORITIES

TO-DO

TIME

DAILIES

MEALS

B

L

D

S

AUGUST / /

S M T W T F S

PRIORITIES

TO-DO

TIME

DAILIES

MEALS

B

L

D

S

AUGUST / /

S M T W T F S

PRIORITIES

TO-DO

TIME

DAILIES

MEALS

B

L

D

S

AUGUST / /

S M T W T F S

PRIORITIES

TO-DO

TIME

DAILIES

MEALS

B

L

D

S

AUGUST / /

S M T W T F S

PRIORITIES

TO-DO

TIME

DAILIES

MEALS

B

L

D

S

AUGUST / /

S M T W T F S

PRIORITIES

TO-DO

TIME

DAILIES

MEALS

B

L

D

S

AUGUST / /

S M T W T F S

PRIORITIES

TO-DO

TIME

DAILIES

MEALS

B

L

D

S

AUGUST / /

S M T W T F S

PRIORITIES

TO-DO

TIME

DAILIES

MEALS

B

L

D

S

AUGUST / /

S M T W T F S

PRIORITIES

TO-DO

TIME

DAILIES

MEALS

B

L

D

S

AUGUST /   /

S M T W T F S

PRIORITIES

TO-DO

TIME

DAILIES

MEALS

B

L

D

S

AUGUST / /

S M T W T F S

PRIORITIES

TO-DO

TIME

DAILIES

MEALS

B

L

D

S

AUGUST /   /

S M T W T F S

PRIORITIES

TO-DO

TIME

DAILIES

MEALS

B

L

D

S

AUGUST / /

S M T W T F S

PRIORITIES

TO-DO

TIME

DAILIES

MEALS

B

L

D

S

AUGUST / /

S M T W T F S

PRIORITIES

TO-DO

TIME

DAILIES

MEALS

B

L

D

S

AUGUST / /

S M T W T F S

PRIORITIES

TO-DO

TIME

DAILIES

MEALS

B

L

D

S

AUGUST / /

S M T W T F S

PRIORITIES

TO-DO

TIME

DAILIES

MEALS

B

L

D

S

AUGUST / /

S M T W T F S

PRIORITIES

TO-DO

TIME

DAILIES

MEALS

B

L

D

S

AUGUST / /

S M T W T F S

PRIORITIES

TO-DO

TIME

DAILIES

MEALS

B

L

D

S

AUGUST / /

S M T W T F S

PRIORITIES

TO-DO

TIME

DAILIES

MEALS

B

L

D

S

AUGUST / /

S M T W T F S

PRIORITIES

TO-DO

TIME

DAILIES

MEALS

B

L

D

S

AUGUST / /

S M T W T F S

PRIORITIES

TO-DO

TIME

DAILIES

MEALS

B

L

D

S

AUGUST / /

S M T W T F S

PRIORITIES

TO-DO

TIME

DAILIES

MEALS

B

L

D

S

AUGUST / /

S M T W T F S

PRIORITIES

TO-DO

TIME

DAILIES

MEALS

B

L

D

S

AUGUST / /

S M T W T F S

PRIORITIES

TO-DO

TIME

DAILIES

MEALS

B

L

D

S

AUGUST / /

S M T W T F S

PRIORITIES

TO-DO

TIME

DAILIES

MEALS

B

L

D

S

AUGUST / /

S M T W T F S

PRIORITIES

TO-DO

TIME

DAILIES

MEALS

B

L

D

S

AUGUST / /

S M T W T F S

PRIORITIES

TO-DO

TIME

DAILIES

MEALS

B

L

D

S

AUGUST REVIEW

Summary of this Month's Accomplishments

SEPTEMBER EXPENSES

EXPENSES	AMOUNT	DATE

SEPTEMBER GOALS

GOALS	DATE	DONE

SEPTEMBER / /

S M T W T F S

PRIORITIES

TO-DO

TIME

DAILIES

MEALS

B

L

D

S

SEPTEMBER / /

S M T W T F S

PRIORITIES

TO-DO

TIME

DAILIES

MEALS

B

L

D

S

SEPTEMBER / /

S M T W T F S

PRIORITIES

TO-DO

TIME

DAILIES

MEALS

B

L

D

S

SEPTEMBER / /

S M T W T F S

PRIORITIES

TO-DO

TIME

DAILIES

MEALS

B

L

D

S

SEPTEMBER / /

S M T W T F S

PRIORITIES

TO-DO

TIME

DAILIES

MEALS

B

L

D

S

SEPTEMBER / /

S M T W T F S

PRIORITIES

TO-DO

TIME

DAILIES

MEALS

B

L

D

S

SEPTEMBER / /

S M T W T F S

PRIORITIES

TO-DO

TIME

DAILIES

MEALS

B

L

D

S

SEPTEMBER / /

S M T W T F S

PRIORITIES

TO-DO

TIME

DAILIES

MEALS

B

L

D

S

SEPTEMBER / /

S M T W T F S

PRIORITIES

TO-DO

TIME

DAILIES

MEALS

B

L

D

S

SEPTEMBER / /

S M T W T F S

PRIORITIES

TO-DO

TIME

DAILIES

MEALS

B

L

D

S

SEPTEMBER / /

S M T W T F S

PRIORITIES

TO-DO

TIME

DAILIES

MEALS

B

L

D

S

SEPTEMBER / /

S M T W T F S

PRIORITIES

TO-DO

TIME

DAILIES

MEALS

B

L

D

S

SEPTEMBER /   /

S M T W T F S

PRIORITIES

TO-DO

TIME

DAILIES

MEALS

B

L

D

S

SEPTEMBER / /

S M T W T F S

PRIORITIES

TO-DO

TIME

DAILIES

MEALS

B

L

D

S

SEPTEMBER / /

S M T W T F S

PRIORITIES

TO-DO

TIME

DAILIES

MEALS

B

L

D

S

SEPTEMBER / /

S M T W T F S

PRIORITIES

TO-DO

TIME

DAILIES

MEALS

B

L

D

S

SEPTEMBER / /

S M T W T F S

PRIORITIES

TO-DO

TIME

DAILIES

MEALS

B

L

D

S

SEPTEMBER / /

S M T W T F S

PRIORITIES

TO-DO

TIME

DAILIES

MEALS

B

L

D

S

SEPTEMBER / /

S M T W T F S

PRIORITIES

TO-DO

TIME

DAILIES

MEALS

B

L

D

S

SEPTEMBER / /

S M T W T F S

PRIORITIES

TO-DO

TIME

DAILIES

MEALS

B

L

D

S

SEPTEMBER / /

S M T W T F S

PRIORITIES

TO-DO

TIME

DAILIES

MEALS

B

L

D

S

SEPTEMBER / /

S M T W T F S

PRIORITIES

TO-DO

TIME

DAILIES

MEALS

B

L

D

S

SEPTEMBER / /

S M T W T F S

PRIORITIES

TO-DO

TIME

DAILIES

MEALS

B

L

D

S

SEPTEMBER / /

S M T W T F S

PRIORITIES

TO-DO

TIME

DAILIES

MEALS

B

L

D

S

SEPTEMBER / /

S M T W T F S

PRIORITIES

TO-DO

TIME

DAILIES

MEALS

B

L

D

S

SEPTEMBER / /

S M T W T F S

PRIORITIES

TO-DO

TIME

DAILIES

MEALS

B

L

D

S

SEPTEMBER / /

S M T W T F S

PRIORITIES

TO-DO

TIME

DAILIES

MEALS

B

L

D

S

SEPTEMBER /   /

S M T W T F S

PRIORITIES

TO-DO

TIME

DAILIES

MEALS

B

L

D

S

SEPTEMBER / /

S M T W T F S

PRIORITIES

TO-DO

TIME

DAILIES

MEALS

B

L

D

S

SEPTEMBER / /

S M T W T F S

PRIORITIES

TO-DO

TIME

DAILIES

MEALS

B

L

D

S

SEPTEMBER REVIEW

Summary of this Month's Accomplishments

OCTOBER EXPENSES

EXPENSES	AMOUNT	DATE

OCTOBER GOALS

GOALS	DATE	DONE

OCTOBER / /

S M T W T F S

PRIORITIES

TO-DO

TIME

DAILIES

MEALS

B

L

D

S

OCTOBER / /

S M T W T F S

PRIORITIES

TO-DO

TIME

DAILIES

MEALS

B

L

D

S

OCTOBER / /

S M T W T F S

PRIORITIES

TO-DO

TIME

DAILIES

MEALS

B

L

D

S

OCTOBER /   /

S M T W T F S

PRIORITIES

TO-DO

TIME

DAILIES

MEALS

B

L

D

S

OCTOBER / /

S M T W T F S

PRIORITIES

TO-DO

TIME

DAILIES

MEALS

B

L

D

S

OCTOBER / /

S M T W T F S

PRIORITIES

TO-DO

TIME

DAILIES

MEALS

B

L

D

S

OCTOBER / /

S M T W T F S

PRIORITIES

TO-DO

TIME

DAILIES

MEALS

B

L

D

S

OCTOBER / /

S M T W T F S

PRIORITIES

TO-DO

TIME

DAILIES

MEALS

B

L

D

S

OCTOBER / /

S M T W T F S

PRIORITIES

TO-DO

TIME

DAILIES

MEALS

B

L

D

S

OCTOBER / /

S M T W T F S

PRIORITIES

TO-DO

TIME

DAILIES

MEALS

B

L

D

S

OCTOBER / /

S M T W T F S

PRIORITIES

TO-DO

TIME

DAILIES

MEALS

B

L

D

S

OCTOBER / /

S M T W T F S

PRIORITIES

TO-DO

TIME

DAILIES

MEALS

B

L

D

S

OCTOBER / /

S M T W T F S

PRIORITIES

TO-DO

TIME

DAILIES

MEALS

B

L

D

S

OCTOBER / /

S M T W T F S

PRIORITIES

TO-DO

TIME

DAILIES

MEALS

B

L

D

S

OCTOBER / /

S M T W T F S

PRIORITIES

TO-DO

TIME

DAILIES

MEALS

B

L

D

S

OCTOBER / /

S M T W T F S

PRIORITIES

TO-DO

TIME

DAILIES

MEALS

B

L

D

S

OCTOBER / /

S M T W T F S

PRIORITIES

TO-DO

TIME

DAILIES

MEALS

B

L

D

S

OCTOBER / /

S M T W T F S

PRIORITIES

TO-DO

TIME

DAILIES

MEALS

B

L

D

S

OCTOBER / /

S M T W T F S

PRIORITIES

TO-DO

TIME

DAILIES

MEALS

B

L

D

S

OCTOBER / /

S M T W T F S

PRIORITIES

TO-DO

TIME

DAILIES

MEALS

B

L

D

S

OCTOBER /   /

S M T W T F S

PRIORITIES

TO-DO

TIME

DAILIES

MEALS

B

L

D

S

OCTOBER / /

S M T W T F S

PRIORITIES

TO-DO

TIME

DAILIES

MEALS

B

L

D

S

OCTOBER / /

S M T W T F S

PRIORITIES

TO-DO

TIME

DAILIES

MEALS

B

L

D

S

OCTOBER / /

S M T W T F S

PRIORITIES

TO-DO

TIME

DAILIES

MEALS

B

L

D

S

OCTOBER / /

S M T W T F S

PRIORITIES

TO-DO

TIME

DAILIES

MEALS

B

L

D

S

OCTOBER / /

S M T W T F S

PRIORITIES

TO-DO

TIME

DAILIES

MEALS

B

L

D

S

OCTOBER /   /

S M T W T F S

PRIORITIES

TO-DO

TIME

DAILIES

MEALS

B

L

D

S

OCTOBER / /

S M T W T F S

PRIORITIES

TO-DO

TIME

DAILIES

MEALS

B

L

D

S

OCTOBER / /

S M T W T F S

PRIORITIES

TO-DO

TIME

DAILIES

MEALS

B

L

D

S

OCTOBER / /

S M T W T F S

PRIORITIES

TO-DO

TIME

DAILIES

MEALS

B

L

D

S

OCTOBER / /

S M T W T F S

PRIORITIES

TO-DO

TIME

DAILIES

MEALS

B

L

D

S

OCTOBER REVIEW

Summary of this Month's Accomplishments

NOVEMBER EXPENSES

EXPENSES	AMOUNT	DATE

NOVEMBER GOALS

GOALS	DATE	DONE

NOVEMBER /   /

S M T W T F S

PRIORITIES

TO-DO

TIME

DAILIES

MEALS

B

L

D

S

NOVEMBER / /

S M T W T F S

PRIORITIES

TO-DO

TIME

DAILIES

MEALS

B

L

D

S

NOVEMBER / /

S M T W T F S

PRIORITIES

TO-DO

TIME

DAILIES

MEALS

B

L

D

S

NOVEMBER / /

S M T W T F S

PRIORITIES

TO-DO

TIME

DAILIES

MEALS

B

L

D

S

NOVEMBER / /

S M T W T F S

PRIORITIES

TO-DO

TIME

DAILIES

MEALS

B

L

D

S

NOVEMBER / /

S M T W T F S

PRIORITIES

TO-DO

TIME

DAILIES

MEALS

B

L

D

S

NOVEMBER /   /

S M T W T F S

PRIORITIES

TO-DO

TIME

DAILIES

MEALS

B

L

D

S

NOVEMBER / /

S M T W T F S

PRIORITIES

TO-DO

TIME

DAILIES

MEALS

B

L

D

S

NOVEMBER / /

S M T W T F S

PRIORITIES

TO-DO

TIME

DAILIES

MEALS

B

L

D

S

NOVEMBER / /

S M T W T F S

PRIORITIES

TO-DO

TIME

DAILIES

MEALS

B

L

D

S

NOVEMBER / /

S M T W T F S

PRIORITIES

TO-DO

TIME

DAILIES

MEALS

B

L

D

S

NOVEMBER / /

S M T W T F S

PRIORITIES

TO-DO

TIME

DAILIES

MEALS

B

L

D

S

NOVEMBER / /

S M T W T F S

PRIORITIES

TO-DO

TIME

DAILIES

MEALS

B

L

D

S

NOVEMBER /   /

S M T W T F S

PRIORITIES

TO-DO

TIME

DAILIES

MEALS

B

L

D

S

NOVEMBER / /

S M T W T F S

PRIORITIES

TO-DO

TIME

DAILIES

MEALS

B

L

D

S

NOVEMBER / /

S M T W T F S

PRIORITIES

TO-DO

TIME

DAILIES

MEALS

B

L

D

S

NOVEMBER /   /

S M T W T F S

PRIORITIES

TO-DO

TIME

DAILIES

MEALS

B

L

D

S

NOVEMBER / /

S M T W T F S

PRIORITIES

TO-DO

TIME

DAILIES

MEALS

B

L

D

S

NOVEMBER / /

S M T W T F S

PRIORITIES

TO-DO

TIME

DAILIES

MEALS

B

L

D

S

NOVEMBER / /

S M T W T F S

PRIORITIES

TO-DO

TIME

DAILIES

MEALS

B

L

D

S

NOVEMBER / /

S M T W T F S

PRIORITIES

TO-DO

TIME

DAILIES

MEALS

B

L

D

S

NOVEMBER / /

S M T W T F S

PRIORITIES

TO-DO

TIME

DAILIES

MEALS

B

L

D

S

NOVEMBER / /

S M T W T F S

PRIORITIES

TO-DO

TIME

DAILIES

MEALS

B

L

D

S

NOVEMBER / /

S M T W T F S

PRIORITIES

TO-DO

TIME

DAILIES

MEALS

B

L

D

S

NOVEMBER / /

S M T W T F S

PRIORITIES

TO-DO

TIME

DAILIES

MEALS

B

L

D

S

NOVEMBER / /

S M T W T F S

PRIORITIES

TO-DO

TIME

DAILIES

MEALS

B

L

D

S

NOVEMBER / /

S M T W T F S

PRIORITIES

TO-DO

TIME

DAILIES

MEALS

B

L

D

S

NOVEMBER / /

S M T W T F S

PRIORITIES

TO-DO

TIME

DAILIES

MEALS

B

L

D

S

NOVEMBER / /

S M T W T F S

PRIORITIES

TO-DO

TIME

DAILIES

MEALS

B

L

D

S

NOVEMBER / /

S M T W T F S

PRIORITIES

TO-DO

TIME

DAILIES

MEALS

B

L

D

S

NOVEMBER REVIEW

Summary of this Month's Accomplishments

DECEMBER EXPENSES

EXPENSES	AMOUNT	DATE

DECEMBER GOALS

GOALS	DATE	DONE

DECEMBER / /

S M T W T F S

PRIORITIES

TO-DO

TIME

DAILIES

MEALS

B

L

D

S

DECEMBER /   /

S M T W T F S

PRIORITIES

TO-DO

TIME

DAILIES

MEALS

B

L

D

S

DECEMBER / /

S M T W T F S

PRIORITIES

TO-DO

TIME

DAILIES

MEALS

B

L

D

S

DECEMBER /   /

S M T W T F S

PRIORITIES

TO-DO

TIME

DAILIES

MEALS

B

L

D

S

DECEMBER /   /

S M T W T F S

PRIORITIES

TO-DO

TIME

DAILIES

MEALS

B

L

D

S

DECEMBER / /

S M T W T F S

PRIORITIES

TO-DO

TIME

DAILIES

MEALS

B

L

D

S

DECEMBER / /

S M T W T F S

PRIORITIES

TO-DO

TIME

DAILIES

MEALS

B

L

D

S

DECEMBER /   /

S M T W T F S

PRIORITIES

TO-DO

TIME

DAILIES

MEALS

B

L

D

S

DECEMBER / /

S M T W T F S

PRIORITIES

TO-DO

TIME

DAILIES

MEALS

B

L

D

S

DECEMBER / /

S M T W T F S

PRIORITIES

TO-DO

TIME

DAILIES

MEALS

B

L

D

S

DECEMBER / /

S M T W T F S

PRIORITIES

TO-DO

TIME

DAILIES

MEALS

B

L

D

S

DECEMBER / /

S M T W T F S

PRIORITIES

TO-DO

TIME

DAILIES

MEALS

B

L

D

S

DECEMBER / /

S M T W T F S

PRIORITIES

TO-DO

TIME

DAILIES

MEALS

B

L

D

S

DECEMBER / /

S M T W T F S

PRIORITIES

TO-DO

TIME

DAILIES

MEALS

B

L

D

S

DECEMBER / /

S M T W T F S

PRIORITIES

TO-DO

TIME

DAILIES

MEALS

B

L

D

S

DECEMBER /   /

S M T W T F S

PRIORITIES

TO-DO

TIME

DAILIES

MEALS

B

L

D

S

DECEMBER / /

S M T W T F S

PRIORITIES

TO-DO

TIME

DAILIES

MEALS

B

L

D

S

DECEMBER / /

S M T W T F S

PRIORITIES

TO-DO

TIME

DAILIES

MEALS

B

L

D

S

DECEMBER / /

S M T W T F S

PRIORITIES

TO-DO

TIME

DAILIES

MEALS

B

L

D

S

DECEMBER /   /

S M T W T F S

PRIORITIES

TO-DO

TIME

DAILIES

MEALS

B

L

D

S

DECEMBER / /

S M T W T F S

PRIORITIES

TO-DO

TIME

DAILIES

MEALS

B

L

D

S

DECEMBER / /

S M T W T F S

PRIORITIES

TO-DO

TIME

DAILIES

MEALS

B

L

D

S

DECEMBER / /

S M T W T F S

PRIORITIES

TO-DO

TIME

DAILIES

MEALS

B

L

D

S

DECEMBER / /

S M T W T F S

PRIORITIES

TO-DO

TIME

DAILIES

MEALS

B

L

D

S

DECEMBER /   /

S M T W T F S

PRIORITIES

TO-DO

TIME

DAILIES

MEALS

B

L

D

S

DECEMBER /   /

S M T W T F S

PRIORITIES

TO-DO

TIME

DAILIES

MEALS

B

L

D

S

DECEMBER / /

S M T W T F S

PRIORITIES

TO-DO

TIME

DAILIES

MEALS

B

L

D

S

DECEMBER / /

S M T W T F S

PRIORITIES

TO-DO

TIME

DAILIES

MEALS

B

L

D

S

DECEMBER / /

S M T W T F S

PRIORITIES

TO-DO

TIME

DAILIES

MEALS

B

L

D

S

DECEMBER /   /

S M T W T F S

PRIORITIES

TO-DO

TIME

DAILIES

MEALS

B

L

D

S

DECEMBER /   /

S M T W T F S

PRIORITIES

TO-DO

TIME

DAILIES

MEALS

B

L

D

S

DECEMBER REVIEW

Summary of this Month's Accomplishments

YEAR REVIEW

Summary of this Year's Accomplishments

YEAR REVIEW

Summary of this Year's Accomplishments

YEAR REVIEW

Summary of this Year's Accomplishments

YEARLY ACHIEVEMENTS AT A GLANCE

Write down all of your Biggest Achievements this Year

JANUARY

FEBRUARY

MARCH

APRIL

MAY

JUNE

JULY

AUGUST

SEPTEMBER

OCTOBER

NOVEMBER

DECEMBER

PEOPLE I MET THIS YEAR

NAME	PLACE	DATE

PEOPLE I MET THIS YEAR

NAME	PLACE	DATE

PEOPLE I MET THIS YEAR

NAME	PLACE	DATE

DEBT AT A GLANCE

Write down the balance of each debt and monitor your progress each month.

1. DEBT: APR EXP.:
2. DEBT: APR EXP.:
3. DEBT: APR EXP.:
4. DEBT: APR EXP.:
5. DEBT: APR EXP.:

JANUARY	FEBRUARY	MARCH

APRIL	MAY	JUNE

JULY	AUGUST	SEPTEMBER

OCTOBER	NOVEMBER	DECEMBER

YEARLY EXPENSES AT A GLANCE

EXPENSES	AMOUNT	DATE

YEARLY EXPENSES AT A GLANCE

EXPENSES	AMOUNT	DATE

NOTES

NOTES

NOTES

Made in the USA
Monee, IL
04 November 2026

67391572R00233